To Trish

Happy 40th Birthday!!

I came across this book + thought of you immediately! Wishing you a very happy day + year! + another 40+ years of being young at heart! :)

We love you!

Love Erin + the Schneider boys :)

Michael Jackson

A Life in the Spotlight

Philip Dodd

Endeavour London Ltd.
21–31 Woodfield Road
London W9 2BA
Fax 44 (0) 20 7579 5710
info@endeavourlondon.com

ISBN: 9781-1-873913-13-0

A catalogue record is available from the British Library

Printed in Italy by Nuovo Istituto Italiano d'Arti Grafiche S.p.A

Art Director: **Ian Denning**
Picture Research: **Jennifer Jeffrey**, **Ben Bonarius**
Project Co-ordinator: **Liz Ihre**
Production: **Mary Osborne**

Acknowledgements

Picture research for this book was directed by Jennifer Jeffrey
with the more than able assistance of Ben Bonarius. Even in
the extraordinarily brief time they had to research, their task
was made much easier by many in the Getty Images world:
Lee Martin, Adrian Murrell, Bob Ahern and Kate Booker,
Getty Images London; Jonathan Hyams and Paul Chesne from
Michael Ochs Archive; Elodie Maillet, David Maskrey and
Matthew Somorjay from Contour by Getty Images; Julian
Ridgway from Redferns; Penny Larson and Nora Cranley from
Getty Images NY and LA respectively

Philip Dodd would like to thank Pam and John Gibbon and
everyone at Bourrat Sud for their forbearance and Pascal, Nadia
and the staff at Campanile Marmande for their gracious help.

Half Title: Michael Jackson at the Nassau Coliseum,
8th November 1979.
EBET ROBERTS/REDFERNS/GETTY IMAGES

Frontispiece: Michael Jackson's chair on the set of
"You Rock My World" promo video, August 2001.
JONATHAN EXLEY/CONTOUR FOR GETTY IMAGES

Right: Michael during the *HIStory* tour, New York, 1997.
DAVE HOGAN/GETTY IMAGES

"I was a
veteran even
before I was
a teenager."

1 Starburst 1958-1974

Michael Jackson's whole life was a stage, and one he started
performing on as a toddler. The promise of his singing voice and
the quality of the dance steps he pitter-pattered round the family's
house prompted his mother Katherine to tell father Joe – already
hard at work welding together his four eldest sons into a group that
could realise his own thwarted musical ambitions – "I think we have
another lead singer". By the time of these 1971 photos, Michael,
at twelve, was a seasoned professional entertainer, the Jackson 5
having signed with the mighty Motown label two years earlier.

Right: Tito, Marlon, Jackie, Michael and Jermaine.

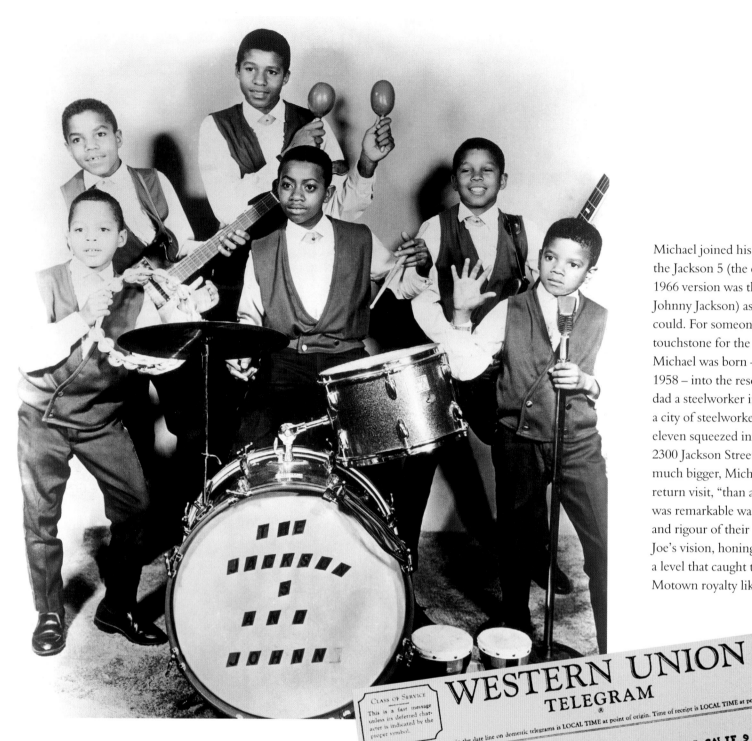

Michael joined his elder siblings in the Jackson 5 (the drummer in this 1966 version was the unrelated Johnny Jackson) as soon as he could. For someone who became a touchstone for the extraordinary, Michael was born – on 29th August 1958 – into the resolutely ordinary: dad a steelworker in Gary, Indiana, a city of steelworkers, his family of eleven squeezed into a house, at 2300 Jackson Street, which was not much bigger, Michael said on a return visit, "than a garage". What was remarkable was the discipline and rigour of their dedication to Joe's vision, honing their talents to a level that caught the eye of Motown royalty like Diana Ross.

Right: As part of the Jackson 5 marketing strategy Berry Gordy and Motown decided that Diana Ross would "discover" the group and she formally introduced them to the public on August 11th, 1969, although interestingly in this telegram from her to Mary Wilson, Michael's age appears to be incorrect.

WESTERN UNION
TELEGRAM

CLASS OF SERVICE
This is a fast message unless its deferred character is indicated by the proper symbol.

SYMBOLS
DL = Day Letter
NL = Night Letter
LT = International Letter Telegram

The filing time shown in the date line on domestic telegrams is LOCAL TIME at point of origin. Time of receipt is LOCAL TIME at point of destination

330P PDT AUG 9 69 LD214
L HDA172 (L BHA083 LY) DF NL PDB FAX BEVERLYHILLS CALIF 9
MISS MARY WILSON
    1820 RISING GLEN HOLLYWOOD CALIF(DY)
PLEASE JOIN ME IN WELCOMING A BRILLIANT MUSICAL GROUP THE JACKSON
FIVE ON MONDAY, AUGUST 11, 6:30 TO 9:30PM AT THE DAISY, 326NORTH
RODEO DRIVE, BEVERLYHILLS THE JACKSON FIVE FEATURING SENSATIONAL
EIGHT-YEAR-OLD LEAD SINGER MICHAEL JACKSON WILL PERFORM LIVE
AT THE PARTY. PLEASE COME AND LISTEN TO THIS FABULOUS NEW MOTOWNROUP
RSVP 275-4588
    DIANE ROSS

The Jackson 5 were signed to Motown in March 1968. Finely tuned and rolled out off what the label's founder Berry Gordy, Jr called his "assembly line", given the patronage of Diana Ross and the benediction of Ed Sullivan, the group burst into national consciousness in late 1969, and how. It was crossover heaven: four singles, four Number Ones: "I Want You Back", "ABC", and "The Love You Save" followed by "I'll Be There". This ballad, which Michael called "our breakthrough record", was a chance for him to move beyond the chirpy bubblegum soul of the first three singles and the dance moves he'd respectfully purloined from the inspirational James Brown.

Success for the Jackson 5 did seem to be as easy as ABC, although the hard graft required was carefully concealed. After such a storming, record-breaking start to the group's career, the natural progression was for Michael, as their front man – front boy, more accurately – to be groomed for solo stardom. "Got To Be There", and "Rockin' Robin", his cover of a Bobby Day track from the 1950s, both reached the Top Five. But it was "Ben", an unlikely choice as the theme tune from a movie about a rat, that gave Michael his first solo Number One in 1972.

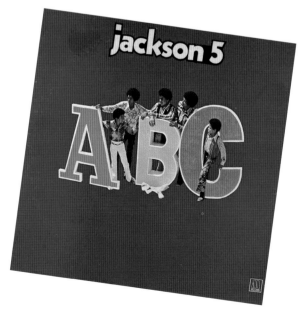

The Jackson 5 cross paths with the Brady Bunch at ABC Studios in July 1971 – this was
an era when TV seemed hooked on shows about families: alongside the Jacksons and
the Bradys, the real-life Osmonds and the invented Partridges. Although two months
later the September issue of *Life* magazine featured the brothers on the front cover at
home "with Mom and Pop", the image of a cosy, normal family life was as artificial as
the cartoon series about them launched by the ABC Network that same month.

"The pros have
told us that no
group has ever
had a better start
than we did.
Ever."

Left: Jermaine, Tito, Michael, Marlon
and Jackie with commemorative
copies of their "Third Album", 1970.

Left: Joe and Katherine Jackson with the five at their home in Encino, 1970.
Above: Janet and Michael 1972.

All families are dysfunctional, the saying goes. The Jacksons spent time together by necessity, probably more than many other families. Michael talked in later years about the complex, volatile and sometimes fractious relationship with his father – he was "always a mystery to me", he said. But despite this and the pressures of feeding the unrelenting demands of the entertainment industry, Michael's bond with and affection for his youngest sister Janet – whose solo success would be second only to Michael's – is obvious. The gentleness of his mother Katherine, a devout Jehovah's Witness, was the glue that kept them all together.

Joe Jackson drove his family hard. "When I found out that my kids were interested in becoming entertainers," he told *Time* magazine, "I really went to work with them. When the other kids would be out on the street playing games, my boys were in the house working." Their Hollywood Hills home had plenty of facilities if they ever found a spare moment to relax – there was a badminton court and archery range too – and made for great photo opportunities.

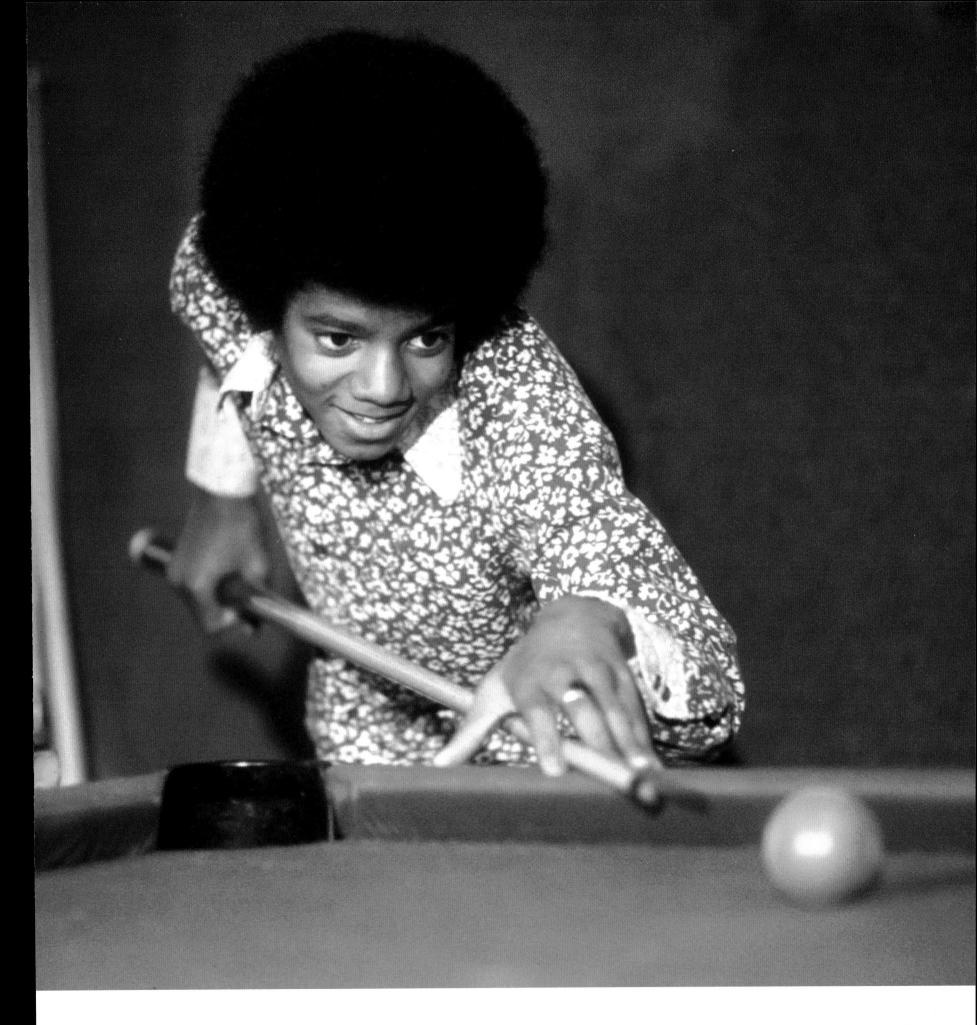

"You don't get to do things that other children get to do, having friends and slumber parties and buddies. There was none of that for me. My brothers were my friends."

Above and right: Michael at home with Marlon, November 1972, during a shoot for black teen magazine *Right On!*

Michael in his element, performing at the Forum in Los Angeles in August 1972, and backstage with Randy and Marlon. Two years earlier, during the first year of Jacksonmania, a show there had had to be cancelled after the audience grew out of control in their over-excitement and rushed forward. The young Michael's natural, seemingly unforced, stage presence was already compelling, even back in 1967 when the group had first appeared at an amateur night in the Apollo Theater in Harlem, the venue of James Brown's classic live album. Reports of Michael's performances there and at the Regal in Chicago had filtered back, via Gladys Knight amongst others, to Motown in Detroit.

A transatlantic flight followed by a press call was a sure sign of international pulling power. The Beatles had caused a furore landing at LaGuardia; the Jacksons flew in the other direction and touched down at Heathrow in October 1972. Their tour schedule included a Royal Command Performance at the London Palladium in the presence of Queen Elizabeth the Queen Mother, where the group's set included Michael's solo hit "Rockin' Robin". He had enjoyed more success as a solo artist in the UK than the group had, and it was thanks to this that the Jackson 5 were mobbed on arrival.

Left: London Palladium, October 1972.
Below, Olympia, Paris, November 1972.

Huge in America, the Jacksons were building an international following. Their late 1972 European tour also took them to the Netherlands, Belgium, Germany and France, and raised their profile in what had been something of a sluggish market in their terms. The following year the Jackson 5 were the first Afro-American act to undertake a nationwide tour of Australia and in 1974 they went to Africa.

Still in his mid-teens, Michael had become a
celebrity in his own right, out with his parents
for the evening, or posing with Donny
Osmond and Partridge Family member Ricky
Segall at the 1974 American Music Awards.
As his personal star continued its ascendancy,
the Jackson 5's fortunes were starting to
wane. Singles like "Little Bitty Pretty One",
"Lookin' Through The Window" and
"Hallelujah Day" had fared poorly by Jackson
standards, and Michael's solo "Morning
Glow" from the musical *Pippin* had suffered
too. A new lease of life was required.

By the mid-70s the Jackson 5 were going through a period of flux. They parted company with Motown in May 1975, although Jermaine remained with the label, a decision not unconnected with his marriage to Berry Gordy's daughter Hazel. Younger brother Randy, who had already appeared with the group on stage, was waiting in the wings to take Jermaine's place. Motown held on to the group's name, forcing them to change to the Jacksons as they joined CBS. But before they left, "Dancing Machine" introduced the world to one of Michael's trademarks, a robotic streetstyle dance move. As Michael said, "It seemed every kid in the United States was doing the Robot."

Right: Backstage at The Forum, Los Angeles, August 1973.
Above: Michael and Randy.

"My brothers and I –
our whole family – were
very proud. We had
created a new sound for
a new decade."

"I'm never pleased
with anything.
I'm a perfectionist.
It's part of who I am."

2 Dancing the Light Fantastic 1975-1982

Just as the Jacksons, minus Jermaine, prepared to quit the Motown
organisation which had launched and nurtured their triumphant early
career, and sought the key to recovering their glory days, so too Michael
readied himself to step away from the midst of the group into his own
limelight and to carve a distinctive, defining and dazzling niche for himself.

Those who met the teenage Michael Jackson offstage
usually reported back that considering the fact he had been
performing with apparently effortless confidence since
he was a child, Michael was still remarkably shy. His voice
hovered just above a whisper. He found it difficult to
make, let alone hold, eye contact. And he seemed most
comfortable in the company of animals and pets, his siblings
– here helping out little sister Janet at the 1975 American
Music Awards – or other youngsters. But his sensitivity
belied a steely determination and an unyielding spirit.

Before Michael could start moulding his own future as a solo artist, there was work to be done reshaping the fortune of the Jacksons, as they were obliged to call themselves in the post-Motown era. A rainbow coalition of soul-pop ambassadors, they headed to Jamaica in 1975, where they were booked to appear with the Wailers at the National Stadium in Kingston Jamaica. Bob Marley was an admirer of the group, and invited them, with mother Katherine, to his home on Hope Road. The hope the Jacksons most wanted to realise was a successful relationship with their new label Epic to send them back to the top of the charts.

Above: The Jackson 5 performing in Jamaica, March 1975, just prior to their move from Motown and Jermaine's departure from the group.

The brothers, posing here with sisters Janet, La Toya and Rebbie, were teamed up by Epic with producers Kenny Gamble and Leon Huff, who had created the "Philly Sound" for the likes of the Three Degrees and Harold Melvin and the Blue Notes. But the first album with Gamble and Huff – *The Jacksons* – never quite lived up to expectations, despite the presence of "Show You The Way To Go". Michael decided to make this a positive experience, learning from Gamble and Huff the craft of structuring a song, knowledge he carefully stowed away for future reference.

Disappointing sales – their second Epic album *Goin' Places* went precisely nowhere – were not perked up even by a TV series, on CBS naturally, filmed at Burbank Studios. The conviction grew among the brothers that they should not only write their own material rather than leaving it up to hired hands, but produce themselves. They struck a deal to do just that with a label equally disappointed in them. It was double or quits roll of the dice.

Left: Randy, La Toya, Marlon, Michael, Janet, Rebbie, Jackie and Tito, November 1976.

Michael's appeal was undiminished. In May 1977, in Memphis, Tennessee, the presence of the Jacksons, specifically Michael, created a mini-riot. Shortly afterwards he was approached by, of all people, Motown Productions via Diana Ross, to appear in the film version of *The Wiz*, a stage musical of Frank L. Baum's *Wizard of Oz* with an all-black cast. Michael would be the Scarecrow to Diana Ross's Dorothy. He said he identified with the confused nature of the character… Certainly he was concerned about his skin – he had typical teenage acne – and the size of his nose.

Left and below: The Jacksons fooling around, New York, 1977.

"I'm crazy for kids and animals and puppies. I love exotic things."

Above and right:
Michael preparing for a
magazine studio shoot
with an assortment of
stuffed animals (**left**),
Los Angeles, July 1978.

For the filming of *The Wiz*, Michael finally left the family home, setting up in an upscale Manhattan apartment with sister La Toya. The movie's director, Sidney Lumet, said Michael was a consummate professional, working flat out on set but partying hard at night. He is seen here with Steve Rubell, owner of Studio 54, the club adored by the disco glitterati, and fellow guests Aerosmith vocalist Steven Tyler and Cherie Currie from the Runaways, and hanging out with Muhammad Ali and his wife at a tennis party.

Left: Michael with Lionel Richie, 1980.
Above: Janet and Michael before the American Music
Awards, Santa Monica Civic Auditorium, January 1977.

The Wiz bombed, and Michael, who had put such effort and faith into
the project, was heartbroken. But out of the failure came one great
connection. The music for the movie had been directed by Quincy
Jones, trumpeter, arranger, record executive and film composer.
The pair clicked, and when Michael's thoughts turned to a solo project,
Quincy, a new mentor to take over from Michael's own father/manager
Joe and Motown's Berry Gordy, was ready, and willing, to help.

Michael's appearance at the first – and perhaps unsurprisingly the last – episode of the Rock'n'Roll Sport Classic in May 1978 was an unlikely affair. Although his brothers were all sporting, he was not in the least. But he was in training, for the new solo album that he started recording at the end of the year.

1978 and 1979 were Michael's
years of destiny, literally so,
with the release of the Jacksons'
album of that name in 1978.
Their gamble had paid off:
it was funky and irresistible,
including Michael and Randy's
"Shake Your Body (Down
To The Ground)" and "Blame
It On The Boogie". The
following year the fruits of
Michael's collaboration with
Quincy Jones – the *Off The
Wall* album – burst into view
like a shooting star. Michael
unveiled a new falsetto register
for his voice to punctuate
the album's intense, but
spontaneous, mood and the
blend of disco, pop, soul and
R&B whisked up by Quincy's
magisterial production.

Michael's songwriting had matured – the first single from *Off The Wall* was his own "Don't Stop 'Til You Get Enough", a US Number One – and his dancing was showcased in an innovative video where he danced with himself in triplicate. He was equally happy to strut on a party dancefloor, here in June 1979 with Tatum O'Neal, with whom he had a "relationship", platonic according to Tatum. They shared the same history of precocious stardom: she'd won an Oscar at the age of nine, starring opposite her father Ryan in *Paper Moon*. "I like her," said Michael, "because she's a survivor."

Along with his sophisticated songwriting (fresh from *Off The Wall*, he had a writing credit on six out of nine of the next Jacksons album *Triumph*) came an elegant, more adult, look: bow tie, dinner jacket, trademark socks and Bass Weejuns. *Off The Wall* produced four US Top Ten singles from one album, the first time any artist had achieved this: "Don't Stop" followed by "Rock With You", "Off The Wall" and "She's Out Of My Life", which came complete with genuine tears for an extra dramatic frisson – Michael broke down on every take.

"When I was little I used to stay with Diana Ross. I never said, but I always had a crush on her."

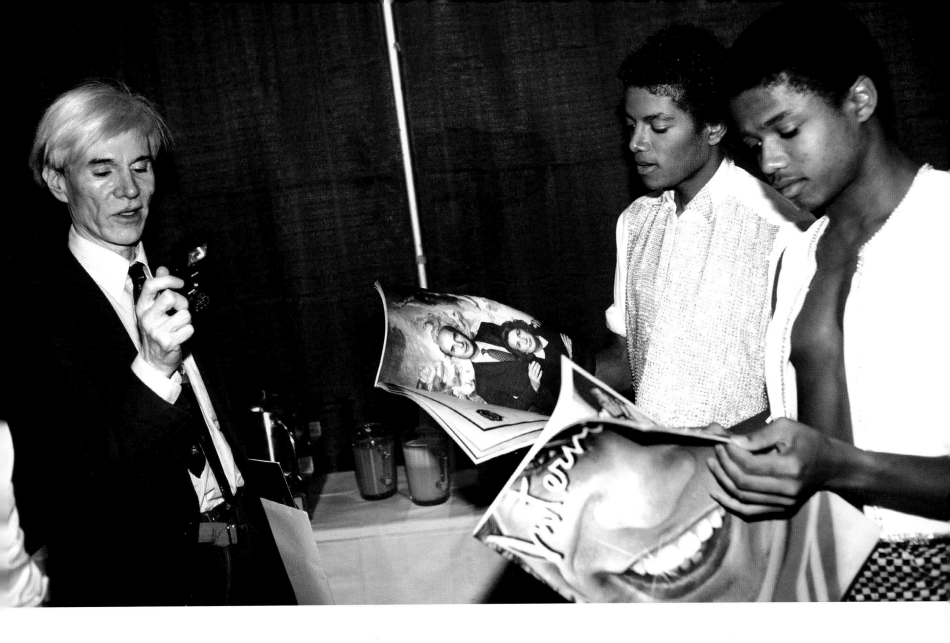

But Michael was not satisfied. Despite the plaudits, the awards, and being feted by the likes of Diana Ross (for whom he wrote and produced "Muscles" in 1981), when the Grammys came round he "only" picked up Best Male R&B Vocal Performance for "Don't Stop". He felt that *Off The Wall* had been snubbed, especially as it had pioneered an unprecedented crossover between the entrenched belief in separate black and white audiences. He was determined that the next album should be impossible to ignore.

Left: Michael with Diana Ross at the American Music Awards, 1981.
Above: Michael and Randy with Andy Warhol backstage during the Jackson 5 *Triumph* Tour, 1981.
Right: Michael with Donna Summer in 1982.

"I wanted to do an
album where every song
was like a hit record."

The recording timetable for the next album, *Thriller*, in 1982 was crazy: eight weeks from start to finish to hit the Christmas market, and the first single – "The Girl Is Mine", a doe-eyed duet with Paul McCartney – was released while the rest of the album was still under construction. Although the single reached Number Two in the US, the choice of song seemed somewhat lame and unremarkable. The fans had no need to be concerned. The best was yet to come.

Michael: **"There's something I've got to tell you."**

Michael's Girl: **"Yes, Michael?"**

Michael: **"I'm not like other guys."** *– Thriller* video

3 Supernova 1983-1990

The fuse of *Thriller*, lit in late 1982 with the release "The Girl Is Mine", initially burned safely and steadily. But come the turn of the year, the sky was spattered with starbursts: a double whammy with "Billie Jean" and "Beat It" topping the charts in rapid succession and Michael's career-changing appearance – one that transformed the music industry along the way – at Motown's 25th anniversary show. Sales of *Thriller* exploded. At one point the album was described as being part of the household furniture. Michael Jackson, it seemed, could moonwalk on water.

Above: Michael in *Thriller* video. **Right**: Performing during *Bad* tour, Japan, 1987.

From hundreds of songs, Quincy and Michael had settled on nine for *Thriller*, of which Michael had written four, including "Billie Jean". Michael's tale of the kind of stalkers he himself had come across, opened with a long slow groove. Quincy wanted to cut it back ("He had an intro you could shave on, it was so long"), but Michael's instincts were spot on. The music was great, darker, funkier, and the videos eye-popping: in "Billie Jean" Michael setting the pavement alight with his dancing, and "Beat It" all *West Side Story*.

Filming "Beat It" video, November 1990.

On top of everything, Michael stunned a huge
TV audience in February 1983. At the tribute for
Motown's quarter century of hit making, the
Jacksons reunited with Jermaine, and then Michael
took a solo spot for "Billie Jean" – what cheek: it
was a CBS, not a Motown, song – and wowed
everyone by combining the moonwalk, a rework of
the street dance move called a backslide, with a
spin and jump up onto his toes, Fred Astaire-like.
Thriller sold a million copies the following week.

Left: Alongside Jane Fonda receiving a Platinum Award for
Thriller, 1983. **Above**: With producer Quincy Jones at the
Grammys, February 1984. **Right**: At the Brit awards with Kim
Wilde, Pete Townshend and Paul McCartney, February 1983.

After all that, Michael – against all his record company's advice – hired John Landis, the director of *An American Werewolf In London*, to craft a $1,000,000 budget, 14-minute film version of *Thriller*, with a "Making Of" video to help fund the unheard-of budget. At the celebrity-attended premiere the audience wanted an encore, but Landis had nothing more to run. "Show the goddamn thing again", yelled Eddie Murphy. Coming out a year after the *Thriller* album, the video sent it stratospheric once again. And although Michael released *Victory* with his brothers, including Jermaine, and toured with them, it was his final outing with the Jacksons. He was out on his own now.

Left: Michael during the Jackson's *Victory* Tour, 1984.

Thriller had produced seven Top Ten singles from one album, a record, and at the 1984 Grammys, Michael collected eight awards, which was another record. But amid all the celebrations, there was a scare that spring. Recording a version of "Billie Jean" for sponsors Pepsi-Cola, Michael's hair caught light from some pyrotechnics, and he was rushed to Cedars-Sinai Medical Center. His scalp was badly scarred, and from then on he started wearing wigs, and relying on painkillers.

Left: Michael and dancer at Pepsi Bottlers Convention, February 1984. **Above**: Being taken to hospital with burns during shooting of Pepsi commercial, 27th January 1984.

Below left: With Cher at *Dreamgirls* party, Los Angeles, 1983.
Below right: At the American Music Awards with Diana Ross, January 1984. **Right**: Michael embraces Liza Minnelli after her concert at the Universal Amphitheatre, Los Angeles, April 1983.

The impact of *Thriller* had placed Michael Jackson at the top of the music business, the first black artist to crossover so completely: the canny use by Quincy Jones of guitarist Eddie Van Halen on "Beat It" legitimized Michael's music to a rock audience. The "King of Pop" tag came soon after, and Michael's access to the higher echelons of the entertainment world proved useful when he co-wrote, with Lionel Richie, "We Are The World" as the USA's Live Aid single.

Michael Jackson found himself being merchandised, waxworked, honoured and memorialised. The boy was still only in his mid-twenties. He was now reaping the financial rewards of *Off The Wall* and *Thriller*, using a large chunk of those rewards to acquire Northern Songs, the publishing company that owned the early Beatles songs. Given the tip-off by Paul McCartney as to how valuable owning publishing rights could be, Macca might be forgiven for being upset that his duetting partner had taken his advice and acquired his heritage.

Opposite left: Michael Jackson doll.
Opposite right: Unveiling his waxwork at Madame Tussaud's, London, March 1985.
Left: Michael receiving an honorary doctorate from the president of Fisk University during the 44th Anniversary celebration of the United Negro College Fund watched by Quincy Jones and Whitney Houston, 10th March 1988.
Below: The Hollywood Walk of Fame.

Now Michael started appearing almost exclusively in settings and costumes that he controlled and styled, sometimes escorting stars like Brooke Shields around town, here with Emmanuel Lewis from the sitcom *Webster*, but increasingly protected and isolated behind the smoked glass barrier of a limousine window. His wealth allowed him to indulge his dreams, but if he had never enjoyed a "normal" childhood, he was slipping into an adulthood that was even more unreal.

"The success of *Thriller* transformed many of my dreams into reality."

MICHAEL JACKSON

BAD
THE WAY
YOU MAKE ME FEEL
SPEED DEMON
LIBERIAN GIRL
JUST GOOD FRIENDS
ANOTHER PART OF ME
MAN IN THE MIRROR
I JUST CAN'T
STOP LOVING YOU
DIRTY DIANA
SMOOTH CRIMINAL

The Thrill Is Back!!
10 Brand New Hits!!!

BAD

He began to demonstrate the eccentricities that would later be seen as early signs of freakishness. He surrounded himself with a menagerie of celebrities and pets – Bubbles the chimpanzee was his most famous animal chum – though he turned this to good use by creating a soft toy range to raise money for charity, as he did diligently throughout his life. It provided some relief to the problem facing him: the difficult, nigh on impossible, task of coming up with a successor to *Thriller*. Having declared he wanted the next album to be "like Tchaikovsky's *Nutcracker Suite*", small wonder it took five years to create and release the follow-up, *Bad*.

While Quincy Jones, co-producing again, was tied up working on the movie of *The Color Purple*, Michael prepared dozens of songs for the new album. All bar two songs were his own, including "I Just Can't Stop Loving You", "Smooth Criminal" and "The Way You Make Me Feel." Prince declined to contribute to the title song. *Bad* had a sharper, more steely soundscape, but some critics thought some formulaic complacency had crept in. Martin Scorsese, though, directing the *Bad* video and, watching Michael dance, saw no stasis, only "quicksilver in motion."

Filming of *Bad* video,
New York, November 1986.

Below: Arriving at Heathrow airport, London
with manager Frank DiLeo, 11th July 1988.
Right: With Princess Diana after his Prince's
Trust concert, Wembley, London, July 1988.

The mercurial star was ready to take his
show on the road, and his first ever solo
world tour was prepared for 1987. Along the
way he came face to face with Diana,
Princess of Wales. This "Princess of Hearts
meets the Prince of Pop" moment was, at the
time, simply wonderful fodder for tabloid
headline writers. Only in retrospect was it a
star-crossed snapshot of two iconic, troubled
and prematurely curtailed lives colliding.

The *Bad* tour lasted over sixteen months, from the opening show in Tokyo in September 1987 to the closer in Los Angeles in January 1989. Over four million people saw Michael on stage in the intervening months, the London leg of the tour delivering a record seven sell-out nights at Wembley Stadium. The fans saw Michael "smooching" on stage with backing singer Tatiana Thumbtzen and pulling a girl from the audience to dance with him on "She's Out Of My Life".

Rumours of Michael's sexuality, or a-sexuality, had been a constant pressure over years. Intensely private, he was puzzled by the huge interest fanned by the lack of an obvious relationship beyond the child stars, show business legends and his private zoo. "I feel like my life is incomplete. I adore family life," he would say, but for now he was "married to my music."

Performing during his *Bad* world tour, 1988.

Below: *Bad* tour, Japan, 1987. **Right**: *Bad* tour, Wembley, London, July 1988 during which Michael breaks a World Record with 504,000 people attending seven sold-out shows.

"My goal in life is to give to the world what I was lucky to receive: the ecstasy of divine union through my music and my dance."

Left: 100 Million sales award, 20th February 1990. **Above**: With President and Mrs. Bush after being honoured as Entertainer of the Decade, 5th April 1990. **Right**: With President and Mrs Reagan, 4th May 1984.

Invited to the White House as a role model for young Americans, the establishment had embraced Michael Jackson, though Nancy Reagan, after husband Ronald gave Michael an award for supporting a campaign against teen drink driving, remarked, "A boy who looks just like a girl, who whispers when he speaks, wears a glove on one hand and sunglasses all the time? I don't know what to make of it."

"Wacko Jacko. Where did that come from? I have a heart. I have feelings. I'm just like anyone. I cut and I bleed."

4 The Twilight Zone

1991-1999

Michael Jackson entered the 1990s following a decade of almost untarnished glory. He had, with Quincy Jones's collaboration, reinvented pop. He had helped start tearing down the Berlin Wall of colour prejudice. And he had made a fabulous fortune. The onus was on him to resist the danger of following his climb to the top of the pedestal with the dramatic fall all the clichés anticipated. Sadly, as he withdrew into his own private world, indications were that his inner demons rather than angels were gaining the upper hand – doubtless one clad in a sequined glove.

Above: Michael visiting Sydney Zoo, November 1996.
Right: Performing at the Brit Awards, London, 19th February 1996.

There were significant changes afoot in Michael's professional life. In 1990 he dispensed with the services of John Branca, the lawyer and business adviser who had negotiated the business deals that made Michael Jackson hugely wealthy, commanding the kind of advance and royalty packages that even other members of the exclusive Superstars Club, like Madonna, could only envy. But that was not enough, and Branca received a curt dismissal in a couriered letter – either Michael's acute shyness revealing itself in an inability to deal with confrontation, or perhaps it was sheer arrogance. His closest musical relationship, with Quincy Jones, had also run its course.

Left: Michael and Madonna at Spago's after the Academy Awards, March 1991.
Above: *Dangerous* album cover, 1991.

Above: Stevie Wonder, Aretha Franklin, Michael and Diana Ross at President Clinton's Inauguration, 17th January 1993.
Below: President Clinton and daughter Chelsea sing along with Michael and Diana Ross at his Inauguration.

Quincy Jones was not involved in the new Michael Jackson album, *Dangerous*, released in November 1991. The new guiding lights were Terry Riley, creator of "new jack swing", brought in to bolster a stronger street sound, and Bruce Bottrell, later to work with Sheryl Crow. The early signs were promising: a single, "Black Or White", with guitar courtesy of Guns N' Roses' Slash, which was Michael's biggest seller since "Billie Jean", its message of racial equality resonated with one presidential candidate in particular.

Michael's fan base was loyal: *Dangerous* sold four million copies in a couple of months. A series of videos featured cameos from his high-profile friends: Macaulay Culkin, Tyra Banks – and the Simpsons – for "Black Or White" (directed, like *Thriller*, by John Landis). Eddie Murphy, Iman and Magic Johnson appeared in Herb Ritts' "Remember The Time", Michael Jordan on "Jam". The *Dangerous* tour ran from June 1992 to November 1993: a visual highlight of the shows was when Michael changed into a silver jumpsuit and, Bond-like, jet-packed offstage. The stunt, devised with David Copperfield, was performed by a double, of course. The often indistinct line between reality and illusion was the one Michael had to walk from now on.

Two weeks after performing at Bill Clinton's Inauguration ball – a platform Michael used to call for a greater commitment to HIV/Aids, then still a sensitive topic – the singer appeared at Super Bowl XXVII. At one point Michael conjured up yet more stunning *trompe-l'oeil* effects before swinging into a four-song set, rounded off by "Heal The World" surrounded by 3,500 children: the hefty profits from the *Dangerous* tour were being diverted to Michael's Heal The World Foundation. The audience for his half-time show, variously estimated as between 120 and 140 million viewers, was famously higher than for the on-field football action either side.

Behind the scenes trouble was brewing. Michael was dealing with allegations about an inappropriate relationship with Jordie Chandler, a boy he had befriended. Elizabeth Taylor defended him on *Oprah*, saying, he was "the least weird man I have ever known". Michael was ploughing ahead with preparations for the ambitious *HIStory* album – 15 hits counterbalanced by 15 new songs, including "You Are Not Alone" – and tour, announced by the modest little wheeze of invading major cities with colossuses representing Michael sporting his favoured militaria look.

2 COMPACT DISC SET

MICHAEL
JACKSON
HIStory
PAST, PRESENT AND FUTURE
BOOK I

Above and Right:
Launching the Michael Jackson *HIStory* statue on the Thames, London, 15th June 1995.

In May 1994 Michael Jackson surprised everyone, and probably himself, by entering the state of matrimony. In a hastily convened ceremony in the Dominican Republic he wed none other than Lisa Marie Presley, daughter of the previous undisputed holder of the title King of Pop. Their marriage made a kind of surreal sense, since both bride and groom had grown up within a bubble of global celebrity and press intrusion. "When you go into his world", Lisa Marie later recalled, "you step into this whole other realm."

Above: Lisa Marie and Michael visit Versailles, 1995.
Left: Appearing in "You Are Not Alone" video.
Right: At the Neverland ranch.

For the time being, the tensions at the heart of Michael's life, unimaginable for the rest of us mere mortals, were, just about, counterbalancing. His professional reputation remained intact, and his performances, here with Slash at the 1995 MTV Video Music Awards, were full of panache and invention. Album sales were strong. But he was carrying the scars of the Jordie Chandler allegations, a sordid affair of rumour, scandalmongering, appallingly bad judgement, greed and humiliation – Michael was photographed naked by the police, anathema to someone so painfully shy and private – out of which no one emerged in a good light, although some emerged substantially richer.

By 1995 Michael was clearly stressed, increasingly dependent on painkillers. His music kept him as sane as he could ever be, but if that ever fell apart, the fragility behind the mask was quite frightening. Even as he performed with Marcel Marceau at the MTV Video Music Awards, the relationship with Lisa Marie Presley was disintegrating. Days before a planned one-off show at New York's Beacon Theater in December 1995, Michael collapsed and was hospitalized but there was no reconciliation. Divorce papers were filed the following month.

With the dust barely settled on the failure of his marriage, Michael plunged back into work, arriving in the *favelas* of Rio de Janeiro to film a video for the single release of "They Don't Care About Us". His penchant for working with the very best directors in the business had not let up: this was a Spike Lee project. However, controversy was now never far away from anything Michael was involved in: the song's original lyric had been rewritten after accusations of anti-Semitism.

"Children are incredible. My most creative moments have almost always come when I am with children."

The public scrutiny of every movement, every appearance, was unrelenting and increasingly negative. A week after the "They Don't Care About Us" shoot, Michael was at Earl's Court in London for the Brit Awards, to receive an Artist Of A Generation award from Bob Geldof. Straightforward stuff, and certainly justified, you might have thought. But as Michael appeared on stage with another children's choir to perform "Earth Song", Pulp frontman Jarvis Cocker interrupted the act, saying he was making a protest about Michael portraying himself as "some kind of Christ-like figure with the power of healing". Jarvis Cocker understood the power of image as well as Michael Jackson. Pulp sales leapt.

Within a year, Michael's private life had taken another unexpected twist. In November 1996 he got married again, to Deborah Rowe, who had formed a bond with him when she was a nurse-cum-receptionist at his dermatologist's – how else could Michael meet a nice girl? Debbie Rowe was five months pregnant at the time of the wedding, and gave birth, in February 1997, to a son called Prince Michael Jackson Jr., the choice of Prince not a sign of self-delusion, but the name of Michael's grandfather and great-grandfather.

Above: Michael with wife Debbie, Paris, 1997, **Right**: *HIStory* tour, Bremen, 1997.

On the *HIStory* tour it was business as (un)usual,
another massive and spectacular show with Michael
moving into *Star Wars* mode – he was a dedicated
fan of the George Lucas movies, and Lucas had
produced Michael's 1986 sci-fi short *Captain Eo*.
An appearance in a pod, wearing a CP3O-style
costume harked back to one of the most persistent
of "Wacko Jacko" stories, that he slept in a hyperbaric
oxygen chamber, a story Michael had helped foster
by releasing photos of himself doing precisely that.

HIStory: Past, Present and Future, Book I, to give the two-disc album the full weight of its portentous title, had become the highest selling multi-disc album ever, racking up more than 20 million units. A highlight was the duet with his sister Janet, now a star in her own right, on "Scream". The tour of the album was equally strong commercially: Michael and his backing band, featuring Jennifer Batten on guitar (she had also accompanied him on both the *Bad* and *Dangerous* tours), played to over four and a half million fans.

As the *HIStory* tour crew prepared to pack up the wardrobe boxes for the final time, the delicate fabric of Michael's offstage life hung in the balance. Although Debbie Rowe had presented her husband with a second child, a daughter called Paris, in April 1998, the couple, who had barely, rarely experienced any semblance of a normal married life together, separated shortly afterwards, although they remained by all accounts on good terms. Michael was left to return home, alone again, to a life away from his fans.

Michael remained committed to charity work. Although he had his own Heal The World Foundation, which had been particularly active during the 1990s in war-riven Sarajevo and post-Ceaucescu Romania, he also supported Nelson Mandela's Children's Fund, the Red Cross, UNESCO and over thirty other charities. The "Michael Jackson And Friends" concert in Seoul in June 1999 – a second event was put on in Munich – continued the good work. Whatever else happened in Michael Jackson's life, his generosity towards the less fortunate was never in doubt.

"People think they know me, but they don't. I am one of the loneliest people on this earth."

5 Fade To Black 2000-2009

As the millennium rolled past, Michael Jackson seemed unable, or unwilling, to buck the trends of the preceding decade. His behaviour was more unpredictable, his musical vision more grandiose, the media backlash more unforgiving. As his skin appeared to turn ever whiter, the shadows surrounding him darkened and deepened – neither was a pretty sight. Yet his true fans, though troubled by what they saw or heard or read, their belief in him sorely tested, stayed remarkably loyal. Their faith was Michael's shining light.

Above: Michael arriving at Santa Barbara County courthouse, 24th March 2005.
Right: At the 2006 World Music Awards, London, 15th November 2006.

For a while things perked up. In 2001, Michael Jackson was more visible than he had been in a long time. He was inducted as a solo artist into the Rock and Roll Hall of Fame, opened the day's trading at NASDAQ, and performed with Justin Timberlake's 'N Sync during that year's MTV Video Awards. In September, a two-night concert at New York's Madison Square Garden celebrated his solo career on the 30th anniversary of the beautiful "Got To Be There", his first single outside the umbrella of the Jackson 5: the brothers were united once again on stage.

The Solo Years event was a true gathering of the clans, and not just the Jacksons. Michael's long-time friends and associates, including Elizabeth Taylor, Macaulay Culkin and Quincy Jones, turned out en masse to share in the festivities. The A-list guest list featured Muhammad Ali and Yoko Ono. And the new generation of younger stars, 'N Sync, Britney Spears, Usher and Destiny's Child, gathered to pay homage to the man who was still for them a master of their craft.

Michael's 30th Anniversary Celebrations, September 2001,
with **below**, Lenny Kravitz and **right**, Britney Spears.

For Britney Spears, the first show, on 7th September 2001, gave her the opportunity to
duet (they sang "The Way You Make Me Feel") with the person she called "an inspiration
throughout my whole life." The following week 9/11 savaged the Manhattan skyline –
in a mood as sombre as four days earlier it had been celebratory, Michael helped organize
a fundraiser in Washington DC, writing and recording the song "What More Can I Give".

As so often, Michael found relief in performance when the rest of his life was in turmoil. In the spring of 2002 he took part in a Democratic National Committee "Night At The Apollo" and *American Bandstand*'s golden jubilee special at a time when he was locked in dispute with his record company, Sony Corp, as CBS Records was now known. Michael claimed they were under-promoting his latest album, *Invincible*, and its ten million sales, healthy by most standards, were viewed as lacklustre by an industry who expected much more.

"I made
a terrible
mistake.
I would never
intentionally
endanger
the lives of
my children."

There were further difficulties
for Michael to overcome.
In November 2002 he had to
testify in the Santa Maria
Superior Court in a wrangle
over alleged breach of contract
with the promoter Marcel
Avram. That, at least, was a
typical entertainment business
dispute. But later that month,
he created self-induced grief
when he appeared on the
balcony of the Adlon Hotel in
Berlin to show fans outside his
new son – Prince Michael II,
a.k.a. "Blanket", born after
artificial insemination of an
unnamed mother – and
hoisted the eight-month-old
baby over the edge of the
balcony. The self-righteous
tabloid scorn was savage.

Below: At the 8th Palm Beach International Film Festival with Brett Ratner, Robert Evans and Al Malnik, 5th April 2003.
Right: With James Brown and La Toya, June 2003

As Michael Jackson was an inspiration to Britney Spears, so James Brown was to Michael. "The greatest education in the world is watching the masters at work," he said, and that spin between the moonwalk and tiptoe stop at the Motown 25th anniversary show was vintage James Brown. A highlight of 2003 should have been spending time with his mentor at the 3rd Annual BET Awards. But if Michael looked drawn, it was because he knew he had just unleashed some of the worst storm clouds of his life.

In February 2003, *Living With Michael Jackson*, a documentary by Martin Bashir, had aired. Michael had granted broad and unprecedented access to Bashir, the BBC journalist whose acclaimed 1995 interview with Diana, Princess of Wales, had created a swell of sympathy for her. Michael, besieged on many fronts, may have hoped for a similar positive reaction. Instead, after being filmed holding hands with 13-year-old Gavin Arvino, and talking on camera about having "slept in a bed with many children", the exact opposite occurred. In November 2003, two months after his 45th birthday, Neverland was raided by the police.

Above and right: Celebrating Michael's 45th birthday at the Orpheum Theatre, Los Angeles, 30th August 2003.
Far right: Michael with Prince Michael I (in scarf) and other children, shopping in the Venetian Hotel, Las Vegas, 27th October 2003.

Neverland was a 2,700-acre estate previously called Sycamore Valley, near Los Olivos, California in Santa Ynez wine country – the landscape that would provide the backdrop for the wine-buff film comedy *Sideways*. The estate had been Michael Jackson's haven and pet project since he bought it in May 1988 for $17 million with the earnings from *Off The Wall* and *Thriller*, and he had spent 15 years fulfilling his own fantasies. Disneyland, Disney World and Universal Studios were still, as an adult, the places where he would choose to spend leisure time. Once his celebrity restricted his ease of movement, he simply built his own theme park.

Visitors to Neverland could catch a train to tour the outer reaches of Michael Jackson's imagination and obsessions. The amusement park had all the requisite features: Ferris wheel, pirate ship and rollercoaster. One of the residents of the zoo was Gypsy, an elephant given to Michael by Elizabeth Taylor, who married Larry Fortensky at Neverland in 1991. There were models of Michael's favourite cartoon characters and, of course, a statue of Peter Pan, the little boy who never grew up, and whose Never-Never-Land the estate was named after.

Once the police arrived at Neverland the spell was broken. Harsh reality had forced its way through the filigree gates. Michael's naïve words in the Martin Bashir documentary led directly to his 2005 trial on charges of molestation, conspiracy to commit child abduction, plying a minor with liquor… Macaulay Culkin appeared in his defence, and called the accusations "absolutely ridiculous". Michael pleaded his innocence. "Lies run sprints", he said, "but the truth runs marathons."

Above: La Toya, Michael and Janet during pre-trial hearing, 16th August 2004.
Right: Michael and his father arriving at Santa Barbara County Courthouse, 1st June 2005.

On 13th June 2005, the jury found
Michael Jackson innocent on all ten
counts against him. Fans who had
waited outside with placards of support –
"Innocent. These eyes don't lie",
"An angel, not the devil" – cheered as
the instinctive showman danced a
few steps on top of a car outside the
courthouse. Almost straight away he
quit America and disappeared from
view, emerging first in Bahrain, where
brother Jermaine had put him in contact
with Sheikh Abdullah bin Hamad Al
Khalifa, before relocating to Ireland.

Michael's health and wealth had taken a battering, his body suffering from vitiligo, the condition he blamed for the lightening of his skin, and there were reports of lupus, emphysema and internal bleeding. Although his Beatles song portfolio was valued at one billion dollars, he was in serious debt, thanks to his extravagant lifestyle, and a stack of legal costs – even the Bahrani sheikh who offered him a refuge after the trial joined the queue of litigants. Public sightings were few and far between. There was a fleeting appearance at the 2006 World Music Awards, when he only sang a few lines of "We Are The World", and forays for shopping trips, sometimes with his kids, when surgical or costume masks were *de rigeur*.

Left: At designer Christian Audigier's 50th Birthday Bash at the Peterson Automative Museum, Los Angeles, 23rd May 2008. **Right**: Michael at a Hollywood antique store, 22nd April 2009.

Michael's financial situation reached its nadir when he defaulted on payments for Neverland, and it seemed he might lose the estate (he never returned there after the trial). In 2009, the auction house Julien's announced a sale of nearly 2,000 of Michael's personal effects at the Beverly Hills Hilton that April. The display of objects was a snapshot of his psyche: stage regalia, gloves, the gates of Neverland, Rolls Royces, miniature electric cars, an arcade's worth of video games and pinball machines. And rare movie memorabilia: an R2D2, Edward Scissorhands' fingers, the actual Oscar that David O. Selznick won for *Gone With The Wind*.

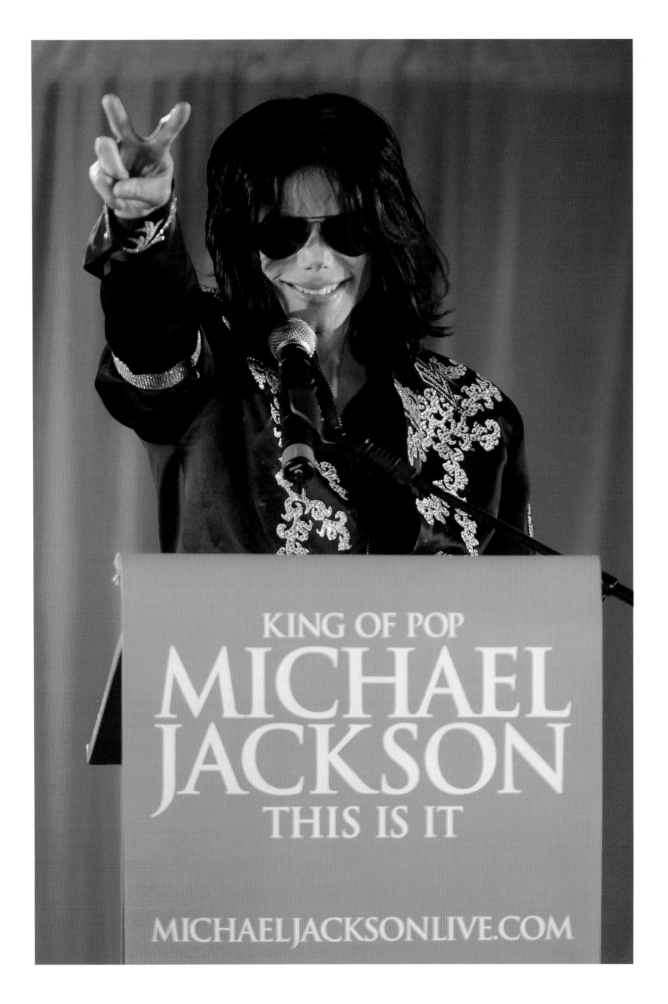

"This is it,
this is really it,
this is the final
curtain call. I'll
see you in July."

Left: Michael at O2 Arena, London
announcing the forthcoming
"This Is It" tour, 5th March 2009.

At the eleventh hour the auction was called off. Michael Jackson had money coming in. During a press conference on 5th March 2009 at London's O2 Arena he had revealed a deal with AEG Live, owners of the Arena, to perform a residency there, just as Prince had done for 21 nights in 2007. Initially ten shows were planned but soon that ramped up to an unlikely 50 – the spirit was willing, the fans were ready, but bookmakers were offering bets on how few of the comeback shows, if any, would ever happen.

Left: Fan Ayesha Obi with the first ticket bought at the O2 Arena for the tour. **Above**: Michael with tour choreographer/director Kenny Ortega, 6th May 2009.

The *This Is It* juggernaut got under way. With dance director Kenny Ortega, Michael oversaw open dance auditions in Los Angeles. Christian Audigier was brought in to design the costumes, Ed Alonzon to devise the illusions and Patrick Woodroffe to supply the light show skills he had honed with Pink Floyd and the Stones. There were concerns about the preparation time (by May some shows were already being shuffled back) and Michael's own readiness – he told fans, "I don't know how I'm going to do 50 shows" – but nevertheless rehearsals at the Staples Center were well underway in late June.

And then it was all over. In retrospect, the death of Michael
Jackson should not have been so very surprising. Health
concerns, severe financial worries threatening an entire lifestyle,
the demands of preparing for a major series of concerts after
a decade in the wings, the sheer weight of expectation building
and building. Yet, when the news came it was a shock. The
first 911 call went out from a rented property in Holmby
Hills at 12.21 pm – "50-year-old male. Not breathing at all".
The ambulance crew found Michael's personal physician trying
to resuscitate him. He was whisked to the Ronald Reagan
UCLA Medical Center where the fight to save him continued.
It was too late. Michael Jackson was pronounced dead at
2.26pm, Pacific Coastal Time, Thursday 25th June 2009.

Digital technology allowed the news to ripple outwards from Los Angeles more quickly than any previous "Where were you when?" moment. Michael's death was Twittered and Facebooked across time zones in a matter of moments. In China and Japan it was a dazed awakening in the early hours of the morning. In London, looking forward to the O2 Arena shows due to start in a matter of days, it was the end of a hot summer's evening. Against the background chatter of news channels dispatching reporters and assembling pundits, and a soundtrack of radio stations lining up back-to-back hits, Michael's fans stood in tearful silence, or quietly prepared to light candles of remembrance.

The memorial service for Michael Jackson was held on Tuesday 7th July, at the same Staples Center where on the very eve of his death, he had been rehearsing for the *This Is It* shows. For someone who had spent the majority of his 50, almost 51, years in the limelight, it seemed oddly fitting that this celebration of his life was also an entertainment special with a global TV and online audience of maybe a billion. Elizabeth Taylor declined to attend ("I cannot be part of the public hoopla. How I feel is between us."), as did Michael's ex-wives. His parents and children, alongside friends and 17,500 fans, waited for the body of their son and father to arrive. A true superstar, he kept everyone waiting 20 minutes, before his brothers entered carrying the gold-plated, rose-laden casket.

At the public memorial service, Staples Center, Los Angeles, 7th July 2009. **Left**: Paris, Prince Michael II and Prince Michael I, **Above**: Rebbie, Janet, Randy, Tito, Marlon, Jackie and Jermaine Jackson.

Among the many tributes that day, three stood out. Berry Gordy remembered the impact of that moonwalk at Motown's 25th anniversary in 1983: "He went into orbit – and never came back down." His 11-year-old daughter Paris expressed her personal loss: "I just wanted to say that ever since I was born, Daddy has been the best father you could ever imagine." And civil rights leader Rev Al Sharpton acknowledged Michael's influence on racial awareness – "He brought down the colour curtain" – before turning to the three children: "There was nothing strange about your Daddy. What was strange was what he had to deal with."

Paris had it right. No one outside his immediate family could begin to imagine the true Michael Jackson. The rest of us only saw, from the outside, the singer, songwriter, dancer, showman. But it is the entertainment he gave us which will be his legacy. The conspiracy theories, the rumours, the speculation about his death can rumble on for years to come. None of that matters. Because although Michael Jackson died on 25th June 2009, his music did not.

"If you enter this world
knowing you are loved and
you leave this world knowing
the same, then everything
that happens in between
can be dealt with."

Left: Michael on the set of music video "Scream", Los Angeles, 1995. **Right**: Michael appearing as an angel for a photo shoot in 1995.

Portraits by Jonathan Exley

Celebrated Hollywood photographer Jonathan Exley worked extensively with Michael Jackson for nearly twelve years. He worked behind the scenes with "The King of Pop" during which time he got to know the reclusive superstar on intimate terms. One of the few people who shared Michael's private family life, he saw a proud and dedicated parent with a penchant for practical jokes and a childlike sense of humour. The photographer was taken aback by the star's sudden death, "Michael Jackson's life took a sudden and unexpected stop. It is very sad", he says, "And right now, for me, I want to remember my friend, this great artist, humanitarian and father."

Michael with his children Prince Michael Jackson Jr., age 5 and Paris Michael Katherine Jackson, age 4, photographed in Los Angeles for *Vibe* Magazine, 17th December 2001.

Left: Marlon Brando and Michael Jackson photographed in Los Angeles for "You Rock My World" promo, August 2001.
Right: Michael with President Bill Clinton, Washington DC, 19th December 2003.

The Jackson family gathered at the Neverland ranch, October 2003. Among those present were Katherine Jackson, Joe Jackson, La Toya Jackson, Michael Jackson, Jermaine Jackson, Paris Michael Katherine Jackson, Prince Michael Joseph Jackson, Prince Michael Jackson II (aka Blanket) and Rebbie Jackson.

A hat, sunglasses and a glove
on display during a public
memorial for Michael Jackson
at The Apollo Theater,
New York City, 30th June 2009.